Masterpieces of Embroidery

FRONTISPIECE: Border: *The Labours of the Months* (detail)
Italy, Seventeenth century
London: Victoria and Albert Museum

One of the most delightful themes for embroidery is The
Labours of the Months. The set from the seventeenth
century, of which this scene of grape harvesting and pressing
is a detail, is in eight panels worked on purple silk net.
Coloured floss silks are used with patterned satin, split, laid
and couching stitches making a very delicate embroidery
which looks almost like a mosaic.

Pamela Clabburn

Masterpieces of
EMBROIDERY

Phaidon Press Limited
Littlegate House, St Ebbe's Street, Oxford
First published 1981
© 1981 Phaidon Press Limited
All rights reserved

Clabburn, Pamela
Masterpieces of embroidery.
1. Embroidery — History
I. Title
746.4'4'09   NK9206
ISBN 0-7148-2046-6

Produced by Graphic Consultants International Pte Ltd
Printed in Singapore

Contents

Acknowledgements

The photographs in this book are reproduced with the kind permission of the museum or collection stated in the caption. Other photographic acknowledgements are as follows: Alinari: 1; Abegg Foundation, Berne: 34; Cooper Bridgeman Library: 22, 24, 49, 54, 70, 71, 75, 77; Studio Rene Basset, Lyon: 36. All black and white photographs of works from the Victoria and Albert Museum, London (with the exception of the frontispiece) are by Carlton Fox Ltd.

Bibliography

Ed. Bridgeman and Drury, *Needlework: An Illustrated History*, Paddington Press Ltd., 1978

G.W. Digby, *Elizabethan Embroidery*, Faber and Faber Ltd., 1963

M. Fitch, *The London Makers of Opus Anglicanum*, London and Middlesex Arch. Soc. Trans. Vol 27, 1976

Nancy Graves Cabot: In Memoriam, Museum of Fine Arts, Boston, 1973

J.L. Nevinson, *Catalogue of English Domestic Embroidery*, H.M.S.O., 1950

C.L. Safford and R. Bishop, *America's Quilts and Coverlets*, E.P. Dutton & Co. Inc., New York, 1972

M. Schuette and S. Muller-Christensen, *The Art of Embroidery*, Thames and Hudson, 1964

P. Wardle, *Guide to English Embroidery*, H.M.S.O., 1970

Introduction

The embroiderer in history

Embroidery is a world-wide art, and like other arts — particularly painting — it has produced styles which reflect both the history of its country of origin and the ideas prevalent among the people at the period in which it was worked. It is a practical as well as a decorative art; the design and workmanship are always relevant to the use of the article. Therefore, as in painting, it is never possible to compare pieces of different times, places and usage, as they will have no relationship to one another. The Bayeux tapestry, made to commemorate a great historical event, cannot be related to the Syon cope, made as a splendid vestment for a prelate two hundred years later. Neither can a piece of embroidery dug from the Paracas Necropolis and worked in southern Peru in the third or fourth century B.C. be compared with a patched and quilted bedcover made in the United States in the nineteenth century. Each is beautiful in its own way, but must be seen in its individual historical context. It is true that fine embroideries can be enjoyed just as fine embroideries; but it is also true that they are immeasurably more interesting when seen as being the products of a particular time and place.

In the history of many countries there have been times when for one reason or another the arts, among them embroidery, have flourished. The reasons for this are not always clear: sometimes it appears to be a stable government, though this was not true of England in the eleventh to the fourteenth centuries when *Opus Anglicanum* flourished; it may be a historical accident, or a coincidental gathering of exciting minds with a searching, inquisitive outlook; or it could be what can only be termed 'spontaneous combustion' — but whatever it is, the results remain for all to see. Central Europe produced wonderful whitework in the fourteenth century; in small, isolated Iceland there was a period in the seventeenth century when unique tapestries and embroideries were worked; there was a workshop in Sicily in the twelfth century where many embroidered masterpieces were made, and so on.

The conditions under which the masterpieces of the past were made were very different from those of today. By far the largest number were worked by professionals — men who had had a long training and had become members of the appropriate guild, working in workshops under a Master. Dr. Marc Fitch has produced evidence which proves that the ecclesiastical embroidery known as *Opus Anglicanum*, worked in England between the eleventh and fourteenth centuries, was — in the late thirteenth century at least — made in London workshops in the neighbourhood of St. Mary Bow. While this had been suspected by embroidery historians for many years, it had always been popularly supposed that ecclesiastical embroideries of this date were worked in convents. Dr. Fitch's researches have proved that the best-known pieces of ecclesiastical embroidery were completely professional work.

It seems that in the Middle Ages the same system was in force all over Europe, though it varied in detail from country to country. Generally the embroiderers mustered in guilds, often joining with the painters in the Guild of St. Luke. This was quite natural, since at this time there was very little specialization in the arts and most embroiderers worked in groups under the direction of a painter. In Belgium, for example, the embroiderers were known as *acu pictores*, painters with the needle; and while they were members of the painters' guild in Antwerp, in Ghent they belonged to the same guild as the makers of quilts and mattresses. In some German towns the embroiderers formed a guild with the braid weavers, in others with the tailors. In Austria the embroiderers with threads belonged to the Guild of St. Luke, while those working with pearls enjoyed free trade, as did the embroiderers of Munster and Nuremburg.

In some places the embroiderers actually worked in a painter's studio, and it was he (often an official Court painter) who drew the design on the linen and directed the work. It was not until the end of the seventeenth century that the painter/embroiderer relationship ceased. In

Italy, Antonio del Pollaiuolo designed a splendid set of vestments for Florence cathedral in the late fifteenth century (Plate 1). Botticelli (1440-1510) supplied cartoons for embroidery, as did Durer (1471-1528), who designed the hood for a cope about 1509. Lesser workshops relied on a series of cartoons or pattern books based on the most popular subjects, which could be used again and again with a little alteration and updating.

Not all large commissions were worked in one place. Patricia Wardle cites the case of a set of vestments made for the Abbey of Averbode in Belgium in 1561-2. The orphreys of the dalmatic were made by Paul van Yeteghem and his sister Edbeth of Lierre, but Gommairs Ververen in Malines worked the face and flesh parts. The matching tunicle orphreys were worked by Pierre and Antoine van Roesbroeck of Lierre, while the frames to the medallions and the borders were worked in the Abbey. The same thing happened in Italy, where the arches that framed the figures drawn by Botticelli were drawn and added by the embroiderers. In the later Middle Ages there was very little Art for Art's Sake — embroidery was a strictly commercial enterprise.

Convents also had their own workshops, sometimes staffed by lay people. In some Orders embroidery was part of the Rule, as in Sweden where St. Birgitta, when she founded Vadstena in 1370, stipulated that part of the nuns' time should be spent in embroidering. In Germany the famous *Opus Teutonicum* or whitework of the Middle Ages was worked mostly in the convents, as was much of the whitework of Switzerland. In Spain the first lay embroiderers of the monastery at Guadelupe learned their trade in the Toledo workshops, after which the monastery workshops became world-famous. It seems that in a number of cases the women tended to do the lighter embroideries such as whitework while the men did the heavier goldwork. This certainly happened in Poland where the Italian queen of Sigismund, Bona Sforza, supervised the workshops and used a team of Italian girls to work the fine linen embroideries, while a team of German men worked with gold and pearls.

Amateur work at its best flourished in households where there was a good and interested needlewoman as *chatelaine* who would be helped by her family, ladies, and servants, working together as a group. In this atmosphere large pieces of domestic embroidery, such as wall hangings and chair and cushion covers, could be made with the less able working the simpler parts. Embroidery in these conditions was a social relaxation enjoyed during long winter evenings, or when bad weather kept people indoors. Many families in remote houses were isolated from friends and neighbours in the winter, and during this shortage of outside interest, the colourful and often romantic themes of embroidery were a godsend to the mundane household.

Trade and conquest

The urge to decorate fabric with thread of any kind from porcupine quills to beaten gold appears to be universal. Except for a few tribes able to dispense with clothing and household goods, all peoples — from the eskimos in the Arctic to the Ethiopians near the Equator — have always felt the need to embellish their clothes and household furnishings. For a thousand years patterns, fabrics and threads have passed between the trading nations and have been assimilated into each culture, until it becomes difficult to tell where a stitch, technique or pattern originated, as in each case it becomes subtly altered to fit another way of thinking. In a few cases a whole idiom has sprung up apparently spontaneously and has then withered away or disappeared, as in the case of the pre-Colombian embroideries found in the Paracas Necropolis in southern Peru.

The greatest influence in the world-wide spread of embroidery has been the Christian Church. We know that there was embroidery before Christ, but the Church has been largely responsible for the exchange of ideas from country to country. The first reason for this is the need the Church has always had for embroidered vestments. From very early days priests and deacons have worn garments decorated with Christian symbols and insignia, and later with naturalistic renderings of scenes from the life of Christ, the Virgin Mary, and Old Testament stories, used to help the illiterate. As the Church gradually grew powerful it acquired gifts for its treasury, its altars, its churches and chapels, and these gifts often took the form of embroidered hangings for the altar and vestments for the clergy — all as rich and as well-executed as possible. This alone gave employment to many embroiderers in the countries of Europe where the Church flourished. It is true to say that in one way and another the Church has been the greatest patron of the arts that the world has known.

The second reason for the influence of the Church on embroidery is its missionary zeal. The Crusades may have been an economic and political disaster for France, Britain and Germany, but they had one unexpected result. A number of men from western Europe, often well-born and well-educated but backward as far as comfortable living was concerned, were thrown into contact with the much more advanced countries of the Mediterranean and Asia Minor. These men saw (generally for the first time) textiles, threads and works of art of a delicacy and beauty which they never could have imagined; and in a number of cases they took back with them, as gifts for their families, small embroideries which must have been a revelation to ordinary French and English women.

The missionary zeal of the Church worked in yet another way. Most convents taught their nuns embroidery, sometimes for the use of their own Order, sometimes for sale to make money to further their work. When these nuns were sent abroad to found convents and schools in various parts of the world they took their skills with them and taught them to the people in their adopted homeland. They started by taking their own fabrics, threads and patterns with them, but before long these supplies were finished. As a sailing ship took months to reach Canada, India or the Philippines, it was obviously no good waiting for, or even sending for, fresh supplies; so they used whatever came to hand, and thus grafted their skills on to native fabrics and threads. This happened particularly in Canada where the Ursuline nuns from France took their own techniques and designs; but they used the moosehair and birchbark that they found in Canada and taught the Indian girls, who understood the native materials, how to work new and attractive designs and use new stitches. Nuns also took their skills to the Philippines but used the very fine local piña cloth (woven from the fibres of pineapple leaves) which is a pale straw colour and as fine as lawn — just right for the drawn fabric stitches that in Europe are worked on muslin or linen lawn.

Nearer our own day came the emergence of Madeira work from the island of Madeira in the Canaries. When nuns settled there in the nineteenth century they took with them the fashionable technique of *broderie anglaise* which was used so much in Europe, particularly on underwear and children's clothes. In Madeira the nuns taught *broderie anglaise* to the peasants, who adapted the technique for use on table- and tray-cloths and all types of household linen. They added a little surface stitchery to the original style, and it became a source of income to the island; it is now known as Madeira work, with its origins all but forgotten.

Trade has played a great part in the movement of embroidery ideas from one part of the world to another. The world centre for all arts was for many centuries the eastern end of the Mediterranean, and here all the trading routes of the world met and crossed. Cotton and flax came from Egypt, gold and silk came along the Silk Road from China. Wool came from the sheep countries of the north, while the art of dyeing, particularly with reds and purples, was one of the oldest of the Near East. From the fifteenth century Italy was the centre of the silk-weaving industry; from there the silks and velvets used for vestments, dress and hangings went to the countries that enriched them with embroidery, particularly England and Germany. England bought much of the linen used for vestments from the Low Countries and her gold thread came from Venice and Cyprus. It was not necessarily made there, but these were two great trading centres, and 'Sipers' gold and Venice gold are frequently mentioned in inventories of the Middle Ages.

Trade also involved the movement from one area to another of goods which acted as patterns, models and inspiration to embroiderers. The formation of the East India Company in 1601 meant that within a few years there was a steady influx of goods, mainly porcelain, from the East. These goods, together with Indian fabrics, became immensely popular in England, Holland and Portugal, and before long resulted in the peculiar phenomenon known as 'chinoiserie'. This can best be described as a foreigner's idea of Eastern art, and gave rise to some of the most charming, if the most fantastic, designs in eighteenth-century embroidery. On counterpanes, dresses, curtains and bedhangings, exotic birds can be seen flying among unreal flowers and foliage; or little men in imaginary Chinese clothes, with very European faces, can be found wandering over little bridges or gazing out of castles shaped like pagodas. To some extent this style from the eighteenth century is still with us in the form of 'willow pattern' china which can be found in many homes today.

A side-effect of this same trade was that sometimes the country that exported the goods has had to modify its designs to suit the taste of its customers. This happened with embroideries exported from India and China. John Irwin has shown that many crewel-work hangings of the seventeenth century, far from being derived from Indian palampores, were in fact embroidered in India in the native idiom from designs and suggestions sent out from England. This is a striking illustration of the way in which trade can give impetus to new ideas. While artistic vision is vital to the production of masterpieces, it is that sometimes despised commodity, trade, which produces the necessary materials, and by the introduction of artefacts from other countries stimulates the artist and gives a fresh vision. This was never more true than it is today, when what might be called the 'ethnic revolution' has made us particularly aware of what other cultures can give us artistically.

Embroidery, with other arts, has been affected over the centuries by conquest — which in the long run has often led to wider trading exchanges. Conquest can be a dire thing, and may stifle all artistic ideas; but on the other hand it can graft new ideas and techniques on to what may have been rather sterile arts. When the Mogul Empire was founded in 1526 northern India was conquered by a race which, though it originally came from central Asia, had assimilated the culture of Persia. The second emperor, Akbar (born in 1542) brought Persian craftsmen to India to collaborate with the Indians in workshops, and from this developed what we now think of as typical Indian embroideries, with Persian motifs hardened by a bolder outline and considerably more detailed naturalism.

Conquest also played its part in shaping the embroideries of central and south-eastern Europe. Between the fourteenth and seventeenth centuries the Turks had control of south-east Europe and the Turkish idiom became imposed on many of the arts. In Hungary, which also had a close connection with Italy, Italian silks and threads were used with many Turkish designs which blended with the native style to produce what we now think of as typical Hungarian work — gay and colourful with peony-type flowers worked in successive rows of satin stitch, producing an effect which resembles the motifs on Turkish ceramics.

Embroidery in Poland was modified through war. While fighting the Turks the Poles captured tents and horse trappings, admired them, and — as well as importing them — persuaded Jewish and Armenian embroiderers to come to Poland and make them there.

Spanish embroidery has always been susceptible to foreign influences. For eight hundred years prior to 1492 the country was dominated by the Moors, who set up embroidery workshops and did many types of work, especially in their favourite colours, black and white. This work, when done on linen using stylized and geometrical motifs, is the 'blackwork' which became so popular in England. It had been known here for a long time but was given fresh impetus by the arrival of a Spanish princess, Catherine of Aragon, who in 1501 came to England to marry Arthur, Prince of Wales, and eventually married Henry VIII. Throughout the sixteenth century it was one of the most popular embroidery styles in England, and is still being worked today. Spain, in her turn, conquered Mexico and parts of South America, with the result that on to her own and the Moorish tradition were grafted Aztec and Inca designs.

From the point of view of theme rather than technique, conquest was the inspiration for two narrative masterpieces: the Bayeux tapestry, which tells the story of the invasion of England by William the Conqueror in 1066; and Overlord, which tells the story of the invasion of the Continent by the Allied Forces in 1944. Both these epic embroideries are the direct result of conquest.

Related to conquest as a catalyst in the production of fine embroideries are political marriages and politics; the Edict of Nantes and its Revocation are prime examples of the way in which a purely political decision in one country can influence the arts in another. In 1598 Henry IV of France signed the Edict, which gave religious freedom to the Huguenots in France. Among the Huguenots were many fine craftsmen including weavers and embroiderers who were now able to settle happily in their native country and work at their trades. In 1685, however, Louis XIV revoked the Edict, which revived religious strife in France and made some 400,000 Huguenots emigrate to Protestant countries, taking their skills with them. This greatly enriched the arts of such countries as England and Holland, while it deprived France of many of her best workers.

Patronage

For the last two hundred years or so embroidery, in common with other arts, has suffered from lack of patronage. Artists and craftsmen cannot live in a vacuum; to do good work they need discriminating customers, who will pay well but make heavy demands on their talents. The patron can be Church, State, wealthy individual or — as is just beginning to happen — industry. In the Middle Ages the Church provided patronage in two ways: either a wealthy foundation would order the vestments or hangings from the embroiderer; or an individual would wish to make a gift in honour of a saint, in thanksgiving, or to placate the Almighty. These gifts would all be as rich and perfect as possible. It was also a time when munificent gifts were exchanged between prelates, reigning monarchs, and the nobility. This all created a demand for superb workmanship and it was this demand that helped to produce *Opus Anglicanum*, and the other embroideries of which we read in wills and inventories but which have disappeared.

After the Reformation the Church ceased to be a patron in Protestant northern Europe but its place was taken by the rising, wealthy middle classes. Sixteenth-century Europe was full of men who were making vast sums of money and who were anxious that the rest of the world should know it. The clothing of both men and women was a background for the conspicuous display of jewels and embroidery, as were the new houses being built all over the country. There was comfort in these new houses: upholstered chairs, cushions, carpets, wall hangings, and beds with embroidered curtains. The use of embroidery in clothes and houses had become a status symbol, and the embroiderers, both professional and amateur, were kept busy.

Today the situation is very different. There are few workshops left, and those that remain work for the great couturiers, the armed forces or the Church. Most embroidery is being worked by the professional who probably teaches as well as accepting a few commissions, or by the amateur who enjoys embroidering articles for her own home.

There has of late been little patronage, but that is slowly changing. A certain amount of work is being commissioned for various churches; and another patron has emerged in the industrialist. Big blocks of offices and new factories need something to soften the rather bleak architecture, and here the artist — whether painter of murals, or embroiderer — comes into his own with large and effective hangings.

Designs and their origins

The sources of embroidery designs were as varied as the themes they portrayed. A noble or royal household would be likely to have its own professional embroiderer/designer. Such a one was Pierre Oudry who was for many years in the service of Mary, Queen of Scots. He drew designs on to linen, outlining them in black silk and leaving it to the Queen to choose her own colours and stitches. Mary also employed, at various times, Ninian Miller who was a Freeman and Guild Brother of Edinburgh, and Charles Plouvart, another Frenchman. Pierre Oudry was a portrait painter, but he did not rate his talents so high that he was not prepared to design for embroidery as well.

Less well-to-do households without a resident designer would use illustrations from books as the source of their designs. Printing started at the end of the fifteenth century and by the middle of the sixteenth century there were editions of the Scriptures and the classics, with illustrations in the form of woodcuts, within the financial reach of many people. *Die Gantze Bibel* was published in 1540 illustrated by Hans Holbein the Younger. One of the woodcuts from this was the inspiration for the whitework cloth (Plate 20) showing Tobias with the Angel. This was a favourite Old Testament story which was embroidered many times.

Another publisher whose cuts were copied many times was Gerard de Jode of Antwerp. In 1585 he published a collection of engravings illustrating scenes from the Old Testament called *Thesaurus sacrarum historicarium Veteris Testamenti*. Plate 8 shows an embroidery adapted from a series of these engravings after the Flemish painter Martin de Vos (1531-1603), Scenes from the Story of Abraham. Here the various separate scenes have been put together to make one embroidered picture.

The use of illustrations to the Scriptures as a basis for design can be cited time and again, and it becomes clear that while the main figures in a number of embroideries can be traced to individual prints and woodcuts, the details were generally altered to fit the contemporary scene. The amateur embroideress — and sometimes the professional as well — felt quite able to cope with draperies and the landscape but needed to have the main structure of the composition worked out. This changing of detail often makes the identification of a particular design difficult; and it is a fascinating and rewarding, if extremely complex, study to try to identify the origins of narrative and incident embroideries (narrative where a whole story is told in a series of pictures, either compressed into a panel or in many scenes; and incident where only one moment in portrayed). Mrs. Cabot of Boston, Mass., (d. 1969) was blessed with a retentive and photographic memory and has put historians in her debt by spending many years pinpointing the connection between prints and embroideries.

The educated minority of the sixteenth- and seventeenth-century population of Europe was very well versed in Greek and Roman literature as well as in many forms of symbolism. They understood allusions which most of us today would find puzzling and, perhaps because far fewer books were available, they read those that they had with care, and knew them well. So it is not surprising to find many sixteenth- and seventeenth-century designs based on classical literature. Bernard Salomon illustrated with woodcuts *La Metamorphose d'Ovide figuree* in 1557, and in the same year *Devises Heroiques* by Paradin was published. In 1658 Francis Cleyn illustrated the Eclogues and Georgics by Virgil, and also the Aeneid; two embroideries taken from these are in National Trust houses — one which is part of the Stoke Edith hangings at Montacute House, and another, worked in 1727 by Julia Calverly, at Wallington.

It was not until the eighteenth century that pastoral romantic scenes became fashionable with a plethora of happy rustics, nymphs, shepherds and shepherdesses, all with the feeling of Marie Antoinette playing in the Trianon. Some of them were taken from a series of pastoral scenes engraved by Claudine Bouzonnet Stella. Later these were modified by Huet into designs for the famous printed cottons, the *toiles de Jouy*. These and many other engravings were not only used for embroideries — they can be found in enamels, porcelain, printed cottons; and in Dresden, for example, anonymous illustrations of the *Commedia del' Arte* were used both for embroidery and for porcelain figures made at the works of Hoechst and Fuerstenberg.

One of the themes (if it can be called a theme) most frequently recurring in the embroideries of virtually all nations of the world is flowers and foliage. They may be worked naturalistically using coloured silks and catching exactly, for all time, the ephemeral blossom; they may be worked in monochrome, showing the beauty of texture by the varied use of stitches; or they may be stylized, flat and formal, making patterns rather than design. In each case one feels that whoever the embroiderer was, he or she loved flowers. Probably the three countries which have shown the most understanding of, and affinity with, flowers in embroidery are Persia, China and England. Each is quite different in interpretation but each exquisite in its own way.

The herbals and collections of flowers published in the sixteenth and seventeenth centuries provided much of the inspiration for English, and through them for American, embroideries. Gerard's *Herball* was published in 1597, and in 1608 Thomas Trevelyan published a *Miscellany* which had many single flower designs as well as some drawn specifically to be worked on men's nightcaps. Crespin de Passe in 1614 published *Hortus Floridus*, a collection of flowers; and Maria Sibylla Merian, a botanical artist and fine embroideress, illustrated a book called *Neues Blumen Buch* — the plates of which were intended for embroidery design. In 1732 Robert Furber, an English nurseryman, wrote *The Flower Garden Dis-*

played which he thought would be useful for many crafts and also 'for Ladies as Patterns for working....'

As well as these books that chiefly contained flowers, there were also many pattern books which illustrated some flowers as well as borders and other patterns. Many of these were aimed at schoolmistresses and were the basis for the samplers worked by young ladies in all European countries. Indeed one, published in Vienna in 1596 with woodcuts by Wolff Luxon, was entitled 'The Pattern Book of authentic Netherlandish stitchery, useful for the well-reputed school-mistress and for the training of the young'.

It is not only the amateur who has lovingly depicted flowers from garden or pattern book; they have also been worked by the highly-skilled professional, as in the gloves of Elizabeth Stuart (Plate 61) while the flower arrangements of Plate 70, worked in the early nineteenth century, are professional French work made to the highest standards.

When flowers are stylized it is because of the limitations of a particular technique. Many pieced patchwork quilts have flowers as their theme under such titles as Cactus Rose, Flower Basket, Flower Garden, North Carolina Lily, or Peony, which are all rigid arrangements; while in the field of applied patchwork the flowers are generally cut from more naturalistically-designed cottons, as in the Westover-Berkeley coverlet (Plate 57). Whoever embroidered the whitework christening gown (Plate 62) used flower motifs more as shapes, to be expressed in various kinds of pulled fabric and surface stitches rather than as natural phenomena; while in the hanging from Russia (Plate 67), round flowers have been used flat to form pattern and show many of the possible variations of decorating a circle.

To see flowers at their most enchanting it is only necessary to look at the portraits of Elizabethan ladies or some of the sixteenth-century coifs and nightcaps in museums. Here flowers riot — sometimes on a curling stem, sometimes with caterpillars, butterflies, dragonflies or small birds, and sometimes showing flower, fruit and seed at the same time. Here more than anywhere else are embroiderers who love flowers.

The craft of embroidery does not lend itself easily to the working of recognizable portraits. It can be, and has been, done — never better than in Overlord, with its stylized but accurate portraits of leaders of the Second World War — but often the only method has seemed to be needle painting as in the portraits by Mary Linwood, copied from paintings, in which each brush stroke has its equivalent stitch. In the eighteenth century the embroideress often gave up, to the extent of painting hands and faces in water-colour on ivory silk while working the draperies in silks or chenille. *Opus Anglicanum* at its best produced some wonderful if expressionless faces, as in the Syon cope (Plate 28) using split stitch for the flesh and enlarging the eyes, making a most acceptable style. Possibly the best portraits known in embroidery are those depicted in the Mass vestments of the Order of the Golden Fleece (Plate 12). In all the vestments, particularly the Dossal, the Saints are worked with such realism that they are probably portraits of real people.

Real or imaginary, stylized or natural, animals have generally been worked with skill, charm and liveliness and have appeared in work of all dates. The animals portrayed in the Middle Ages are seldom domestic, with the exception of the horse, and include legendary beasts such as the unicorn and the gryphon with the stag, lion and eagle, all shown as vigorous, lively and alert.

The sixteenth-century embroideress had at her disposal the first few of a continuing run of bestiaries and natural history books. Conrad Gesner in 1555 published his *Icones Animalium* which went into several editions and was translated and plagiarized by Topsell and others. It had many clear woodcuts which were very suitable for translation into needlework and which can be identified in work by Mary, Queen of Scots, and many others.

Later, pattern books as well as natural history books contained animals for the embroideress to copy. The animals in seventeenth-century embroideries are far more domestic and have a gentleness not seen earlier. Lions are lying down, stags are standing quietly and rabbits gaze out of burrows; and by the eighteenth century, sheep graze on every hillside. This lack of vigour was due, in part, to the use of samplers and small panels as training for the young; so in domestic embroideries, at least, there was a watering-down of design.

A type of design that is common all over the world is the geometrical and purely ornamental which merges into the abstract. Innumerable craftsmen, past and present, have been fascinated by the working-out of complex patterns. That this fascination still continues is evident when so much patchwork, quilting, canvas work and collage is being done at the present. It may be an escape from the rigours of draughtsmanship but it has a special discipline which, in many cases, is being brilliantly carried out.

Pattern without any representational motifs has been used by most nations at various times, but never more than by Moslem countries. The strict Mohammedan believes that any man who takes it upon himself to emulate God by making an image of any living thing will, on the Day of Judgement, have to give that image life, and if he cannot do so will have to give his own life in exchange. So the strict Moslem, be he artist, embroiderer or other craftsman, must content himself with pattern. To the Arabs of the past this was probably no hardship as they were, in the Middle Ages, the foremost mathematicians in the world, and much of their pattern is based on geometrical figures, rather than on natural form as in so many other countries. This interest and skill with abstract design spread from Arab countries into Spain; and from there transmuted, but not essentially changed, it spread to other countries and gave rise to the superb blackwork of the sixteenth century.

Other nations have also been concerned with pattern, particularly the various Indian tribes of America. In New Mexico the Cuna Indians work their *molas* using a reverse appliqué technique making a curved design of several bright colours. Ribbonwork, beadwork and quill-work are done by many Indian tribes, worked in pattern with the occasional very stylized representational motif.

An entirely different kind of pattern was part of the Italian Renaissance when swirling arabesques, allied to foliage reduced to nothing more than a curved stem with a swelling for a leaf, were embroidered on many articles, often in goldwork. This type of ornamental pattern spread from Italy all over Europe (see cover).

Pattern took yet another form in America and England in the nineteenth century with patchwork and quilting. Here the design evolved in most cases from the few pieces of fabric obtainable and the necessity to make something charming to alleviate a rather drab existence. From this it became more involved as fabrics became more readily available, though it is a matter of individual preference between the multicoloured, intricate designs and plainer ones — Amish quilts, for example.

Quilting as a technique has been concerned both with stylized representation and pure pattern. Plain wadded quilts are usually repetitive in pattern, corded quilting is often a mixture, while Italian quilting and trapunto are more often than not representational.

Although pattern books from the sixteenth century onwards have usually included border designs and small abstract patterns, there have been many other available sources; among them mosaics, tiles, pavements, iron-work, architectural details, carvings, frets from Greek vases, and mummy cases. Embroiderers in every country in the world have been quick to make use of the innumerable forms of pattern they see around them, adapting them to their chosen techniques.

Modern embroidery

It is difficult to write of embroidery today as it is too recent to be put into historical perspective; and as with many other arts, especially since 1945, it has been moving very fast in many directions. So fast, in fact, that at times the scene has looked chaotic, which always happens when one stands too close.

Today embroiderers seem to be divided into two completely different camps. In one are the highly articulate and lively-minded trend-setters and the trend-followers, and in the other are the far more numerous but less adventurous, who practise and enjoy the well-tried traditional techniques.

From the beginning of the century and particularly for the last thirty years the trend-setters have mostly been women who have had a general art school training and who look on embroidery as one discipline among many others. Sometimes they have trained as painters and have then decided that they prefer to work with fabric and thread rather than with canvas and brush. This means that they have the approach of a painter to the craft rather than that of an embroideress. Now that a university degree can be obtained in embroidery there are many college students experimenting with all the possibilities, not only of needle and thread, but of dye, paint, glue, wire and many other things that ingenuity might suggest. This is obviously what students should be doing, but sometimes it seems that they are pushing embroidery past the frontiers of the craft and ignoring the basic definition, 'the art of ornamenting material with needlework'.

Many of these students become teachers, and pass on the up-to-date theory that ideas are more important than techniques, creation is all, and that so long as there is self-expression any means will do if it produces the desired effect. However there is no question but that this insistence on experimentation and ideas has made the whole concept of embroidery far more lively than it was before the War.

In the second camp are the many who realize that they are not artists, and who do not want so much to express themselves as to make attractive articles for themselves, their home and their children. To them embroidery is not an art-form but a useful and creative relaxation. As the articles they want to make must withstand wear, they are interested in learning the techniques that will make curtains, cushions, handbags, dresses or whatever, wear well and keep looking fresh and well-made. Not for them are the endless panels, wall-hangings and boxes, but more practical objects; and it must be admitted that at the moment they are not well served or helped. However there are welcome signs that more teachers are now willing to teach basic techniques on which they can build.

In the sphere of ecclesiastical embroidery there has been a very fresh and invigorating wind blowing, and many beautiful and technically excellent vestments have been made, though perhaps not always with a complete understanding of the liturgy and rituals of the various Churches. Here again, ideas have sometimes won against more sober realities. Much of the credit for the enormous vitality and interest of current church embroidery must go to Beryl Dean, who has taught so well at Hammersmith College of Art. She is also a practising embroideress with many superbly-executed commissions to her credit and has involved many of her students in her work, so that they have learned practical difficulties at first hand and have a clear idea of the large technical armoury which is required in this branch of work, not to mention the physical stamina needed.

The making of kneelers for churches large and small has been an interesting and worthwhile post-War development. The idea was originated by that great embroideress and teacher, Louisa Pesel, who before the War gathered a band of workers together to make kneelers to her design for Winchester Cathedral. This was taken up by many parishes after the War, and it would now be hard to count the number which have been made. Generally it has been a team effort led by an embroideress with infinite patience and a love and knowledge of canvas work. Daphne Harmer has masterminded kneelers in St. Paul's and Norwich Cathedrals, Lady Maufe those in Guildford Cathedral, and the list could go on almost indefinitely.

This has had several, perhaps unexpected, results. It has fostered a sense of pride in churches with the idea that each and every member of the parish could contribute, even if they themselves did not use the church for worship; it has beautified the churches and given them a cared-for look; and often it has brought people who may never have used needle and thread before to realize the immense satisfaction that can be got from canvas work.

Pat Russell is another embroideress who has come to needle and thread from another discipline, in her case that of calligraphy. She is fascinated by lettering and its use in embroidery; and few would disagree that in this branch a fresh approach, especially with regard to church embroidery, was necessary. She has taught the modern generation a whole new concept of the use of lettering as part of modern design.

Modern technology has made possible embroidery worked wholly or partially by machine. It is not so long ago that the idea of doing embroidery in any way other than by hand was anathema; but now, largely because of several first-class exponents such as Joy Clucas, it has become not only usual but acceptable as a technique in itself. Not everyone does it well and it is sometimes used just as a time-saver rather than as an integral part of a piece of work, but more and more the two methods are being combined with excellent results.

One of the big advantages of modern embroidery is that when it can be seen, it is in the setting for which it was designed. The reverse is that as it has not yet got into museums, and small pieces at least are generally in people's homes, it is not easy to find. Much modern chuch work can only be seen on special occasions, so the interested onlooker has to be content with exhibitions where it is not always possible to get a clear idea of how the piece will appear in use. It is well worth remembering when looking at embroidery in museums, however well displayed, that it is always out of context and so does not show to the best advantage. The movement of dress, the stirring and the folds of bed and window curtains, and the curve of cushions, give a very different look to the decoration used.

What of the future? Will the two camps eventually fuse into one recognizable trend? Will those who are intent on raising the status of embroidery into an accepted art form ignore the claims of those who have not creative ability but a love of stitchery? One can only hope that there will be a helping hand from the artists to the needlewomen, as there always was in the past.

1: *Salome with the head of St. John the Baptist.* Italy, 1466-1479
Florence: Museo di S. Maria del Fiore

This incident is one of twenty-seven scenes from the Life of St. John the Baptist, designed by Antonio del Pollaiuolo. The set was commissioned by the Merchants Guild of Florence and was incorporated in a set of vestments to be used on special occasions. In 1730 the scenes were detached from the vestments and are now seen individually.

This is one of the embroideries designed by a painter and worked under his direction. The greater part of the panel is worked in *or nué* where horizontal lines of gold thread, sometimes single and sometimes double, are laid and sewn down with different-coloured silks.

2: Hanging (detail). India: Punjab, eighteenth century
London: Victoria and Albert Museum

3: *The Malterer hanging* (detail). Upper Rhine, 1310-1320
Freiburg: Augustinermuseum

This long narrative embroidery from Chamba in the Punjab immediately invites comparison with the Bayeux tapestry (plates 9 and 10) though the source of the inspiration was very different. While the Bayeux tapestry is a factual account of a historical happening, Indian *rumals* or hangings were worked by eighteenth-century embroideresses, based on legends and epics idealizing the warriors of an earlier time. This particular *rumal* represents the battle between the Pandavas and the Kauravas.

Like the Bayeux tapestry worked six or seven hundred years earlier, however, the hanging uses the minimum of stitches and the interest comes from the vitality of the design. The hanging is 10 m long and 76 cm high.

The Malterer hanging may be considered either as a narrative or a series of incidents. In quatrefoils it shows the evil consequences of earthly love as personified by Samson and Delilah; Virgil and the daughter of the Emperor Augustus; Iwein and Laudine; and, in this illustration, Phyllis and Aristotle. The hanging has, at the ends, the arms of the Malterer family, and it was given by them to the Convent of St. Catherine at Freiburg im Breisgau where Anna Malterer was a nun.

It was worked between 1310 and 1320 with wool on linen. The use of irregular, close couching with a little stem stitch for the outlines and draperies, makes an excellent medium for the theme.

4 (above): *Overlord*. England, 1968-1973
London: Whitbread's Brewery, Chilswell Street

Although they were worked nine hundred years apart, there is great similarity between the Bayeux tapestry (plates 9 and 10) and Overlord. The first tells the vivid story of the Norman Conquest culminating in the Battle of Hastings.

The Overlord embroidery was commissioned by Lord Dulverton, designed by Sandra Lawrence, worked by twenty-three girls at the Royal School of Needlework, and has now been presented to the nation. It relates the epic events of the Second World War culminating in the Normandy landings of 1944 (the code name for which was Overlord). It is made up of 34 separate panels each 240 × 90 cm, and is 13 m longer than the Bayeux tapestry.

It is worked mainly in applique and the graphic details were supervised by a panel of experts from the three Services who ensured complete accuracy on every point.

5 (left): *The Story of Joseph* (detail). Ontario, Canada, late 1860s
Royal Ontario Museum

6 (above): *Guicciardini or Tristram quilt* (detail). *c.* 1400, Sicily
London: Victoria and Albert Museum

Quilting is a technique which does not come readily to mind when one thinks of ways of interpreting a narrative, but in at least two cases — the story of Tristram (Plate 6) and the story of Joseph — it has been outstandingly successful.

In The Story of Joseph, twelve separate scenes have been worked symmetrically over the quilt, each scene having an arc of explanatory lettering over it. The scenes and borders are applied with coloured cottons in trapunto, and the ground is meticulously worked in fine running stitch. In a piece such as this, where the colour and the design catch the eye, it is easy to overlook the background of fine running stitch which is such an important part of the complete work.

The Guicciardini or the Tristram quilt has at some time in the past been mutilated, and now one part is in the Victoria and Albert Museum while a smaller piece is in the Museo Nazionale in Florence, and another piece is missing. The quilt originally measured about 476 cm square with a wide border. The panels and the border tell the story of Tristram, the knight who won back the kingdom of Cornwall for his uncle King Mark, from the Irish king. Each scene has its accompanying inscription in Sicilian.

The quilt when first worked must have been superb. The technique used is trapunto, which does not seem the obvious choice for narrative embroidery, but how well it has succeeded!

7 (left): Table carpet. England, sixteenth century
Chicago: Art Institute of Chicago

This is a carpet meant for an almost square table, with a
central design that can be looked at from either end.
Interesting plant forms are encased in hexagonal frames of
cable twist on a dark blue ground. In contrast the border
consists of a series of vignettes taken from the Scriptures.

As with so many needlework pictures, these scenes are
derived from the prints of the time. The Sacrifice of Isaac,
for example, comes from the same source as that in plate 8.

8 (above): *Scenes from the Story of Abraham*. England,
seventeenth century
New York: Metropolitan Museum of Art (gift of Irwin
Untermyer)

This panel is a perfect example of how well the needlewoman
of the seventeenth century could adapt an illustration to her
own purpose. Here, in one large embroidery, 91 cm long and
worked in tent stitch, are arranged three prints from the
Thesaurus sacrarum historiarum Veteris Testamenti published
by Gerard de Jode in Antwerp in 1585. The engravings by
Gerard de Jode were after different masters, and those which
make up this panel are after Martin de Vos (1531-1603).

9 and 10: *Bayeux tapestry* (detail). England, *c.* 1077
Bayeux: Musée de la Reine Mathilde

Little is known about the making of this important piece of
embroidery, which is the earliest known example of crewel
work. Seventy metres long and 50 cm wide, it tells in vivid
and graphic detail the story of the Norman Conquest.

It is generally accepted that the work was commissioned by
Bishop Odo, half-brother to William, and worked within ten
years of the Conquest, probably at Canterbury. The stitches
used are few and simple: laid and couched work, with stem
stitch for the outlines; but the mastery with which they are
combined, together with the extremely lively interpretation of
the drawing, prove that this was not a new technique.

HIC EST
VVILT
DVX

11: *The Bischofszell hanging*.
Switzerland, *c.* 1525
Basel: Historisches Museum

The embroidery known as the Bischofszell hanging, worked about 1525, is unique in that it is an animated landscape with an accurate representation of the town of Bischofszell in the background.

The whole amazing scene is worked in crewel wools in very few colours: green, light and dark brown, red, blue and white, on a dark blue-green woollen fabric; using only two stitches, couching and running. The embroidery measures 175 × 290 cm and is an object lesson in the importance of only using a few colours and stitches for a work full of incident.

12: *Vestments of the Order of the Golden Fleece* (detail of Dossal). Netherlands, probably Brussels, second half of the fifteenth century Vienna: Schatzkammer

The Mercy Seat is a very small part of a set of embroideries known as the Vestments of the Order of the Golden Fleece. It was commissioned by Duke Philip of Burgundy, who founded the Order in 1429, but were probably originally intended for his own chapel and later presented to the Order.

Gold threads and jewels are used, together with many shades of silk. Most of the architectural details and the draperies are in *or nué*, with the flesh and hair worked in split stitch. The look of sorrow on the face of God the Father as he holds the body of His dead Son is most striking and should be compared with the faces in the Syon cope, worked about 150 years earlier but also using split stitch (Plate 28).

13: *Rupertsberg altar frontal*. Rhineland, 1200-1230
Brussels: Musées Royaux d'Art et d'Histoire

In Romanesque Germany, embroidery on linen worked with wool or linen threads was more common than rich work on silk using gold threads. The few exceptions include the Halberstadt chasuble and the Rupertsberg frontal. This is worked on a plum-coloured silk twill using gold and silver threads and pale silks, in stem and satin stitches. The frontal may be dated by the presence of the prostrate figure at the bottom left, named Siegfried, who was Archbishop of Mainz between 1201 and 1230.

The drawing may be faulty and out of scale, and perhaps the workmanship is not as perfect as in some other embroideries of this date; but seldom have stitches expressed emotions so beautifully.

14: *The Judgment of Solomon*. England, late sixteenth century
The National Trust: Hardwick Hall

One of the Bible stories that caught the imagination of the sixteenth and seventeenth century embroideress was the Judgement of Solomon, a story especially suited to fine embroidery in petit point. The long cushion in Hardwick Hall, recorded in the inventory of 1601 as being in one of the windows of the Long Gallery, is as good an example of late sixteenth-century embroidery as it is possible to find, and is quite obviously professional work — probably commissioned by the builder of Hardwick, the redoubtable Elizabeth, Countess of Shrewsbury.

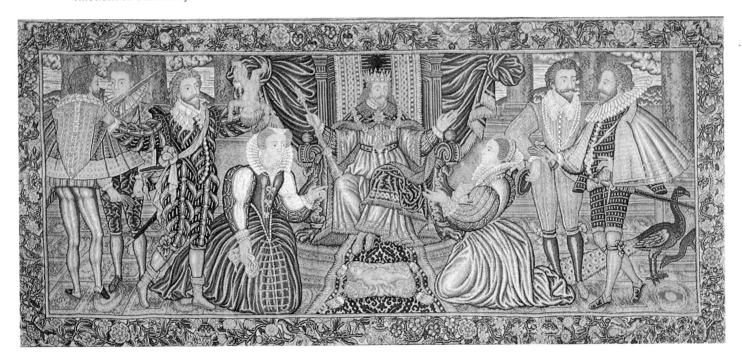

15: Orphrey of a chasuble. Bohemia, 1350-1400
Brno: Moravska Galerie

In spite of having been mutilated, this remains a beautiful and impassioned embroidery. The figure of Christ is emaciated and the features are altogether stronger and less refined than was general in works from further West. They suggest the carpenter rather than the visionary. It is the figures at the foot of the Cross which are so unforgettable; the Virgin Mary half-fainting, being held by St. John the Evangelist and the other Mary, while Mary Magdalene raises her clasped hands in anguish. The ground of the orphrey is of couched gold with most of the embroidery in split stitch, with some *or nué*, a rare technique in Bohemia at this date.

16: *The Weekly Wash*. Switzerland, 1556
Zurich: Schweizerisches Landemuseum

In Switzerland, after the decline of the tapestry-weaving trade, embroideries worked in wool were made to be used as hangings in place of tapestries. In England tent stitch was the generally accepted medium for these hangings but in Switzerland Kloster or convent stitch — a form of couching — was more widely used. Some of these embroideries in wool were small, like this one which gives a wonderfully accurate picture of the laundry maids coming out from the castle into the fields to do the washing.

17 (left): *The Annunciation*. England, 1970
Windsor Castle: The Rutland Chantry, St. George's Chapel

This striking interpretation of the Annunciation is far away in time and style from the other versions (plates 18 and 19) but equally effective. It was designed and worked by Beryl Dean as one of a group of New Testament themes for the Rutland Chantry of St. George's Chapel, Windsor.

Here all the interest centres on the wondering figure of a very young girl sitting on a bank of lilies. The implication is that the angelic visitor was a thought rather than a Being — suggested by the hovering wings. The fabrics and threads are modern and include lurex and leather with pulled and drawn work, appliqué and gold work, on a ground of linen woven with lurex.

18 (above): *The Annunciation*. Coptic, seventh to eight century
Victoria and Albert Museum

The early Egyptian Christians known as the Copts were wonderful weavers, but were not so renowned for their embroidery. This roundel, however, is considered to be Coptic, and represents the Annuciation. It is far removed from the much more sentimental German portrayal (plate 19) and is nearer in spirit to the modern version (plate 17). It is embroidered with a shiny silk thread on linen using split, satin, cross and couched stitches.

31

19 (above): *The Annunciation*. Munich, *c*. 1620
Munich: Residenzmuseum

Here is an altar frontal of superb workmanship and sense of
design — almost with a sense of theatre, in the smoke clouds
which surround the angel and the dove! The main design is in
fine tent stitch, with the flesh parts worked in satin and chain
stitch on white taffeta and then applied.

The perspective of the altar, tiled floor, and window has
strong affinities with Dutch paintings of the seventeenth
century. It was embroidered for the Reichs Kapelle of the
Residenz in Munich and is believed to be after a design by the
Court Painter, Peter Candid.

20: *Tobias and the Angel* (detail). Switzerland, 1563
Basel: Historisches Museum

In 1540 *Die Gantze Bibel* (The Whole Bible) was published in
Zurich with woodcut illustrations by Hans Holbein the
Younger. It was an illustration from that work which was
adapted by the embroiderer of this roundel, and forms the
central motif in a white linen cloth, the rest of which is
covered with coiling sprays of flowers and leaves.

21 (right): *Icon of St. George*. Constantinople, 1729
Athens: Benaki Museum

The embroidered icon of the Eastern church, like the painted
icon, is a representation of a saint or sacred person, which
may in itself be venerated. Embroidered icons are less
common than painted, but among them is this one of St.
George, worked in 1729 by a lady known as the Nun Agatha,
in Constantinople. It is worked in silks and metal threads on
a red silk ground, with the horse in silver. Although, as in all
icons, there is little expression on the face, and it appears to
be a peaceful scene instead of what must have been a bloody
battle, the workmanship is marvellous.

Portrait

22: Roundel: *St. Luke.* Italy, *c.* 1522
Cortona: Treasury of San Francesco

This superbly embroidered roundel represents St. Luke with
his symbol, the bull, and is part of a superfrontal. This, in
turn, is part of a set of vestments made for Cardinal Silvio
Passerini between 1517 and 1526 and presented to the
Cathedral of Cortona. The vestments were designed by the
painters Andrea del Sarto (1486-1530) and Rafaellino del
Garbo (1466-*c.* 1527).

   The work is in *or nué* and the differing distances between
the couching stitches, giving a tiny or a larger glint of gold,
can be clearly seen in the red folds at the bottom of the
roundel and on the back of the book.

23: Altar frontal (detail): *Christ
before Pilate.* Austria, 1340-50
Berne: Bernisches Historisches
Museum

This frontal came from the Convent
of Konigsfelden in Austria and is
mentioned in the inventory drawn up
in 1357. The portraiture is superb, as
much in the grouping and stance of
the figures as in the expression of the
faces. Pilate sits in a relaxed judicial
attitude — interested but non-
committal. In the tight-knit group is
a tired, haggard, despondent Christ.
One soldier is laughing and mocking,
while the other, of whom little more
than the eyes can be seen, is clearly
wondering who this Man is. The
foremost soldier with hand on hip is
obviously bored. It is the priest
haranguing Pilate who animates the
group, while the still figure of Christ
dominates it.

34

24: Altar frontal (detail): *Lady Stafford*. England, 1535-1555
London: Victoria and Albert Museum

The frontal of which this is a detail has on one side the portrait of Ralph Nevill, Fourth Earl of Westmoreland, with his seven sons; and on the other that of Lady Catherine Stafford and her thirteen daughters. They were married in 1523.

The embroidery is worked on linen using split, brick and satin stitches, with couched and raised work in metal threads, which is then applied on to velvet.

25: Mantle (detail). Nazca, Peru, c. A.D. 500
Providence: Rhode Island School of Design

Embroideries from the Paracas Necropolis and from the
slightly later Nazca culture in Peru date from about A.D.
100-900. Most of the embroideries were found wrapped
round the mummy-figures which had been preserved in the
hot, dry sand of the region, and from the fact that some of
the embroideries were unfinished it has been deduced that the
textiles were woven and worked especially for the burials.

The stitches used are an even counted-thread version of
stemstitch worked along the warp or weft of the fabric,
various buttonhole stitches, darning, and double-running.

26: *Portrait of three ladies*. England, mid-seventeenth century
London: Victoria and Albert Museum

This beautifully worked panel is typical of one type of mid-seventeenth century English embroidery in its combination of silk, metal threads and spangles, density of design, and use of flowers and fruit to fill any vacant spaces.

It probably represents three sisters, as the features and hair styles are very similar but the headgear, collars and jewellery are different; and it also seems likely that the lady on the right married into the peerage, as she is wearing a coronet.

27: *The Concert*. France, 1896-98
Copenhagen: Kunstindustrimuseum

This wall hanging was designed by Aristide Maillol
(1861-1944), a French sculptor who specialized in the
female nude. The designer's interests are clearly
shown, as although the figures are clothed in the
voluminous dresses of the late 1890s the lines of the
bodies are distinct; and the centre figure, at least,
might well be sculpted.

   The hanging has been chiefly worked in horizontal
lines of satin stitch. Some couching and chain stitch
have been added to form the shapes, but the main
stitching lines are horizontal with the strong tone
contrasts producing a very harmonious whole.

28: *The Syon cope* (detail). England, 1300-1320
London: Victoria and Albert Museum

The cope of which this is a detail was worked in the
style known as *Opus Anglicanum*, is probably the
most famous of all medieval embroideries. It shows
fourteen scenes from the life of Christ and the
apostles, each in its own barbed quatrefoil shape: this
detail portrays Christ with doubting Thomas.

   In the Syon cope are all the best attributes of *Opus
Anglicanum*: lively drawing which tells a complete
story economically and clearly; the use of split stitch
for details such as face and hands, which was
generally worked in a spiral on the cheeks, giving
slight modelling to the face; and the use of underside
couching for holding down metal threads in pattern.
The latter point is the main reason why so much *Opus
Anglicanum* is in comparatively good condition
today.

29: Altar frontal: *St. George and the Dragon* (detail). Catalonia, *c.* 1460
Barcelona: Case de la Disputacion, Capilla de San Jorge

This altar frontal was designed and worked in Catalonia by Antonio Sadorni. St. George fights the dragon over a ground covered with skulls and bones, watched by the terrified Princess. To the left are the town ramparts crowded with watching citizens, as seen in this detail. Their emotions are clearly expressed: the king horrified, the queen anguished, and the rest all pressing forward for as close a view as possible, even to the lady apparently more interested in the king than in the fight.

Animal

30: Wall hanging. Iceland, fourteenth century
Copenhagen: Nationalmuseum

Iceland has, for most of her history, been under the
suzerainty of Norway and Denmark, but though her arts have
been influenced by those two countries they have preserved a
very individual flavour. In particular, her embroideries have
been vigorous and often unique in conception.

The hanging illustrated comes from the church of Hvau
and is both simple and effective. The background fabric is a
black woollen stuff and the design has been left in reserve.
The white background is worked in wool using a laid and
couched technique which was very popular in Iceland, known
as *refilsaumur*, while the motifs are outlined in a thicker
couched thread.

31: Tablecloth (detail). Switzerland, fourteenth century
Basel: Historisches Museum

This cloth is worked on white linen with a white linen thread
and is a superb example of the type of work for which
Switzerland has always been famous — whitework, or linen
embroidery. The detail shown epitomizes this type of work
with the minimum number of stitches used — in the whole
cloth only satin, plait, eyelet and brick stitches are found to
be necessary.

The gryphon (left) shows clearly that vital, lively drawing
together with meticulous workmanship is often more effective
than a great number of stitches and colours.

32: Crewel work hanging (detail). England, *c.* 1675
Berne: Abegg Foundation

This hanging consists of 49 joined borderless rectangles of
which six are shown. Crewel work designs at this date were
likely to consist of a large tree with out-of-scale leaves and
flowers rising from small hillocks, with a stag and a lion at
each side. Here, however, is something quite different,
worked on a blue twill ground using many coloured wools,
but only long and short and satin stitches. The prancing
horse; the pelican in its piety with, unusually, a fledgling
under its tail; and the birds — all recognizable species —
mobbing the owl, point to a draughtsman who knew and
loved the animal world.

33 (above): *Orpheus and the Animals* (detail). Italy, *c*. 1500
Hamburg: Museum für Kunst und Gewerbe

It is very salutary to realize that perfection of design and
workmanship were quite usual by 1500, when this tablecloth
was embroidered in Italy. The ground fabric is fine white
linen and the design is worked in satin stitch which is, like the
Chinese satin stitch, reversible. In fact, in its use of the fine
blank line to define shape and movement, this piece has an
affinity with Chinese work, but there the resemblance ends.
The design is all European and the designer, apart from being
a superb draughtsman, must have had a very strong sense of
humour, something too often lacking in embroidery.

34 (right): Dossal. Probably Sicily, early thirteenth century
Assisi: San Francesco Treasury

This dossal was given to the Basilica of San Francesco by an
Imperator Graecorum, thought to be Baldwin II (1229-37),
and has been there ever since.

The ground fabric is yellow silk twill worked in couched
gold thread, giving a truly magnificent effect. It might be
expected that the overall appearance could be a little flat and
static even though brilliant, but the aggressive pose of the
animals keeps interest vividly alive. A comparison can be
made with the equally vital gryphons of the Swiss tablecloth
(plate 31), again worked in monochrome but far from dull.

35 (above): *The Fruiting Tree*. England, first half
seventeenth century
New York: Metropolitan Museum of Art (gift of Irwin
Untermyer)

This is one of the most charming of English seventeenth-
century panels. The design indicates the contemporary
interest in tree grafting, though no-one would be likely to
manage strawberries, acorns, cherries, passion fruit, pears,
quinces and lemons all together on one tree! It also is a lesson
in balance. Like most embroideresses of that period, the
maker of this work disliked having any spaces in her design
and has little feeling for scale, but every flower, leaf, bird and
animal is neither crowded nor isolated; and she has framed
her panel with the sky at the top and the River of Life at the
bottom.

36 (right): Panel. Japan, probably early nineteenth century
Lyons: Musée des Tissus

A wonderful piece of the most delicate stitchery, this shows
Japanese embroidery at its enchanting best. Working with
silks on satin, the embroiderer has shown an almost fairytale
scene of the little animal sitting on the ground gazing at the
full moon.

The work is particularly memorable for the way in which
textures have been indicated on a completely flat surface
using only flat stitches and one type of thread. The fuzziness
of the clouds drifting over the moon, the sharp clarity of the
grasses, and the softness of the fur are perfectly rendered.

48

37 (left): Court robe. China, late nineteenth century
London: Victoria and Albert Museum

The robe illustrated is believed to have been made at the end
of the nineteenth century for the last Empress Dowager Tz'u
Hsi, and is of yellow satin embroidered in coloured silks, seed
pearls and coral beads.

Beauty of form and colour was not enough for the
Chinese. There also had to be incorporated into the design
the symbols which, like the emblems of sixteenth-century
England, could be 'read' by the initiated. In this case apart
from the pair of dragons, the pair of temple vases, the sacred
axe, the bat (signifying happiness), the water weed, the bird
and the mountains can all be identified.

38 (above): Linen cloth. South Germany, sixteenth century
Munich: Bayerisches Nationalmuseum

The sixteenth century was the great age of symbolism, a time
when men and women understood or enjoyed puzzling out
allegories and subtle, hidden meanings in conversation,
literature and art.

The cloth illustrated depicts the heavenly bodies, with the
signs of the zodiac on the perimeter. The ground is light blue
linen and the stitchery, all in white linen thread, uses a wide
range of surface stitches for its effect. The vigorous drawing
is in the style of the followers of Hans Holbein the Younger.

39 (left): Rug. Indo-Portuguese, 1580-1640
Paris: Musée des Arts Decoratifs

During the late sixteenth and seventeenth centuries in India a great change in the arts of the country was taking place. The change started with the Mogul emperors bringing Persian craftsmen to India; and it coincided with the influx of foreigners wanting to trade, notably the Portuguese, British and French. The result of this Western interest was that in a number of cases Indian craftsmen worked foreign designs which they translated into their own idiom, or they adapted their own designs to suit their foreign customers.

This silk rug is a case in point, and is a mixture of the Indian and the Portuguese. The centre shows a double-headed eagle and crown, which places the date of the rug between 1580, when Philip of Spain incorporated Portugal and her dominions under the Spanish crown, and 1640 when Portugal recovered her independence.

40 (above): *The Circus*. U.S.A., 1929
New York: Metropolitan Museum of Art (gift of Irwin Untermyer)

The Circus, designed and worked by Marguerite Zorach, is in coloured wools on unbleached linen using many stitches but with single feather stitch predominating. Although in a rectangular frame, the design is based on a circle with the tiger arched over the starred ball as a centrepiece.

As in the panel by Rebecca Crompton (plate 72) the stitches used have underlined the design. All flesh parts of faces and limbs, as well as other items, have been worked in rows of feather stitch — not a stitch normally associated with figure embroidery.

Geometrical

41 (left): Openwork hanging. Iran, nineteenth century
Paris: Musée de l'Homme

42 (above): Patchwork quilt. England, *c.* 1803
London: Victoria and Albert Museum

This type of openwork hanging, so effective in its simplicity, is used in religious ceremonies in Muslim countries to separate men from women. It is, in fact, an embroidered window.

    The hanging comes from the Shiraz district of Iran, about half way down the Persian Gulf and a considerable distance from India; but the design is very similar to the mosaic wall pattern on the south gateway to the tomb of the Emperor Akbar, which was built between 1605 and 1627 at Sikandra in India. This is not surprising as many designs in India were originated by Persian craftsmen.

This quilt may be fairly accurately dated to about 1803 by the medallions round the border, which show military and domestic scenes, and by the centre scene which is thought to represent one of the two volunteer reviews made by George III in October 1803. The whole design is both unusual and individual with the sun and the moon as well as the central motifs superimposed on the ground rosettes, of which there are no fewer than 314. Each of the rosettes was pieced together in a great variety of designs and then applied on to the ground.

53

43 (above): Cover. North-west Persia, sixteenth or
seventeenth century
London: Victoria and Albert Museum

This cover should be compared with the one illustrated in
plate 44, as it comes from the same region of north-west
Persia and they were both worked at much the same date.
The main difference is that while the other is worked in cross
stitch, this one is worked in double darning, which shows
how suitable either stitch can be for this type of work. Again
the design is very closely allied to those of the so-called
Dragon carpets from the eastern Caucasus.

44 (right): Cover. North-west
Persia, seventeenth century
London: Victoria and Albert
Museum

In north-west Persia in the sixteenth
and seventeenth centuries designs for
the staple industry, carpet-making,
and those for embroidery, were very
similar as both crafts were often
pursued in the same house. This
illustration which might well be of a
carpet is, in fact, of a divan cover
worked in cross stitch with coloured
silks on a cotton ground. The
design, based on natural forms, is so
stylized as to be almost non-
representational.

45: Table carpet. England, mid-sixteenth century London: Victoria and Albert Museum

Carpets imported from the Caucasus in the sixteenth century were rare and tremendously expensive — far too expensive to be trodden on — and so were generally used as table carpets instead of foot carpets. Because of their value they began to be copied by English embroiderers, both professional and amateur.

This English carpet is worked in cross stitch and long-armed cross stitch, and the large octagons, based on Caucasian designs, are worked alternately in dark blue and pink. The design of the border with its interlaced strapwork is based on cufic script, a form of writing which takes its name from Cufam, a city near Babylon which was a great seat of Mohammedan learning.

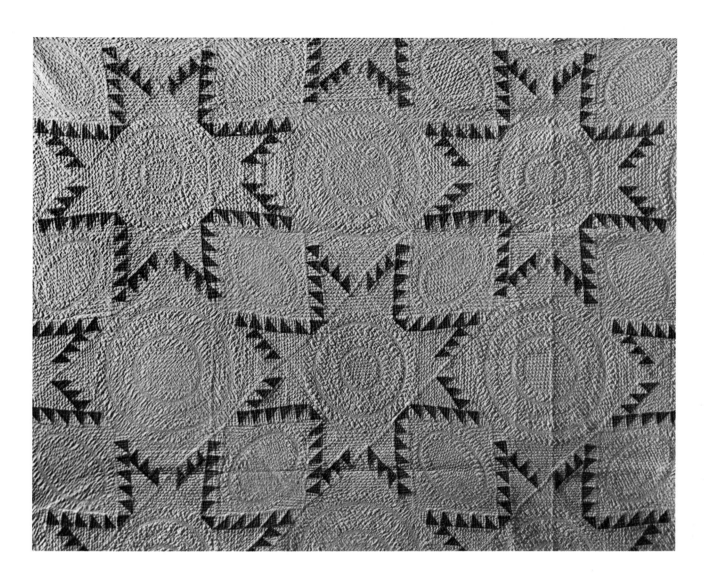

46 (above): *Sawtooth Star* (detail). Michigan, U.S.A., *c.* 1876
Dearborn: Henry Ford Museum

Among the hundreds of patchwork quilts made in the United
States and in Britain in the nineteenth century, it is difficult
to choose a masterpiece. The spread illustrated is not, at first
sight, one of the most spectacular, but it is one that should
appeal to all needlewomen. The pattern is slight but the skill
lies in the quilting which is incredibly fine, and in contrast to
the main design is worked in a series of circles and ovals.

47 (right): Coat. France, 1923-4
Vienna: Collection Anna Lula Praun

Sonia Delaunay, who designed this coat, was a great
influence on the decorative arts during the first half of the
twentieth century. A Russian, she married the French painter
Robert Delaunay in 1910 and thereafter lived and worked
chiefly in France, either with him or on her own. She was
trained as a painter but also worked on bookbindings and
fabrics, and in the theatre, films, and fashion design.
    This coat comes into the last category. It is wool embroi-
dered and has the low waist of 1923-4. The striking design
with its strong tonal value, ranging from cream to black
through shades of brown and dark red, makes it a garment
that would be as wearable today as fifty years ago.

Ornamental

48 (left): Chasuble. Germany, 1629-47
Munich: Bayerisches Nationalmuseum

This chasuble is worked on crimson satin in a mixture of metal threads and coloured silks. The back of the chasuble is divided into three by two narrow borders, and the two outside panels are nearly identical with strapwork in couched gold and formal flower shapes in gold basketwork. The centre panel is rather less formal, with large naturalistic flowers. At the bottom of the panel are the arms of Casimir Anselm of Mainz, Elector between 1629 and 1647, which date the work.

49 (right): Hanging: *The Artichoke* England, *c.* 1875
London: Victoria and Albert Museum

Morris embroideries come between the formal cross and tent stitch of Berlin wool work, and the later teachings of the Glasgow School and Mrs. Christie who emphasized the use of varied stitches to interpret a design. The Morris movement between the two brought freedom of design and execution with a limited use of stitches. Most of the designs are based on natural forms worked into a symmetrical flowing whole, often strongly reminiscent of Italian velvets. The Artichoke designed by Morris himself and worked by Mrs. Godman with crewel wools on linen, is typical of the style.

51: Crib quilt. New England, U.S.A., c. 1820
Dearborn: Henry Ford Museum

Trapunto is a type of wadded quilting where two layers of fabric — the under much more loosely woven than the upper — are stitched together in pattern. On completion, some or all parts of the design have wool poked into them from the back, with the result that some of the design may be flat while other parts are slightly raised. In capable hands this can produce a lovely effect, with the beauty obtained from the play of light and shade on the white cotton top.

50 (left): Table cover. Sweden, 1630
Stockholm: Nordiska Museet

The table cover commemorates the marriage of Count Gustav Horn to Christina Oxenstierna in 1630. The ground is blue taffeta, with the design applied in black velvet outlined with yellow silk thread so tightly sewn down that it resembles yellow beads.

In technique this piece can be compared with the funeral pall from Freiburg (plate 52) worked approximately 150 years earlier, but the result is very different, with a design far removed from the herbal-type plant forms of the pall.

52 (right): Funeral pall (detail). Upper Rhine, late fifteenth century
Freiburg: Augustinermuseum

This funeral pall is a triumph of pure pattern. It was worked in the late fifteenth century, probably in or for the Convent of Adelhausen near Freiburg on the Upper Rhine, and consists of squares of black woollen cloth sewn together. Each square is covered with a different pattern of applied white woollen twill cloth edged with leather strips, originally gilded and silvered.

The feeling which runs through most of the patterns is one of enclosure and interdependence. Could it be a reflection of the cloistered life — that though the individual grows he is still dependent upon and surrounded by others? This work has particular individuality.

Floral

53: Bed furniture. North America, *c.* 1745
York, Maine: Old Gaol Museum

This is one of the best known sets of American crewelwork, believed to have been entirely designed and worked by Mary Bulman to occupy herself while her husband was serving as a surgeon at the Siege of Louisberg. The verses round the valance are from *Meditation in a Grove* by Isaac Watts.

American crewel work was modelled on that worked in England in the seventeenth century but is much lighter in weight with more space between the motifs. Cotton and silk thread is often used as well as wool, and the ground fabric, instead of being the union twill so well known in England, is generally a linen homespun.

54: Bed furnishings. England, 1717
Barnard Castle: The Bowes Museum

During the first half of the eighteenth century a series of very sumptuous bed furnishings was made for some of the homes of the English aristocracy. The set illustrated is typical, with the usual basket of flowers as the basis of the design. The baskets, which were worked first and then applied, are embroidered with gold thread using string padding to give a basket-like effect, and the flowers are worked in natural coloured filoselle silks using mainly long and short stitch.

55: Bed rug. East coast U.S.A., 1808
New York: Metropolitan Museum of Art, Rogers Fund, 1913

Bed rugs are particularly interesting as they are found only in
New England on the east coast of the United States. They
may have a stitched pile or may be worked in chain stitch, but
whichever technique is used the rug is worked on a burlap
(hessian) base, generally in wools, the embroidery always

covering the ground fabric completely. Designs are bold, and
the stitching always follows the outline of the pattern with
only a few shades of colour.

The rug illustrated is signed MB dated 1808, and worked in
plush stitch. It seems likely that this design came from some
pattern book as there is another rug with a very similar
design, dated 1807, in the Shelburne Museum.

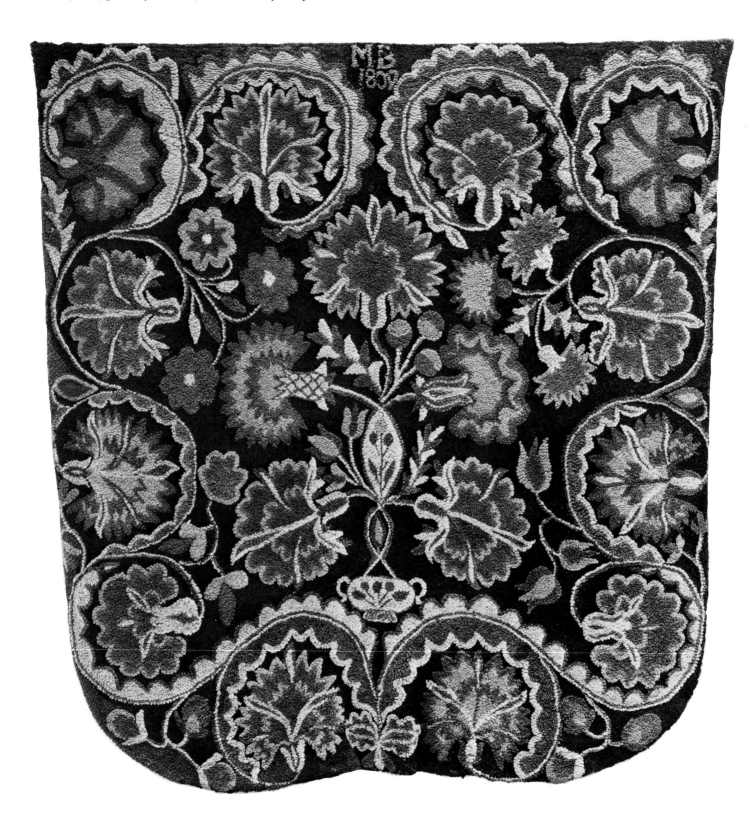

56: Wool bedcover. U.S.A., *c.* 1760
Hartford: Wadsworth Atheneum

In most of the United States in the eighteenth and early nineteenth centuries, embroidery took second place to patchwork and quilting in making articles for the home. The pioneers moving westward had few fabrics and threads, and used what little they had by piecing and quilting with endless patience. On the eastern seaboard, though most threads and fabrics had to be imported, it was possible to embroider domestic articles to add colour and gaiety to the home.

The wool bedcover illustrated was worked by Harriet Dunbar about 1760 on a black twilled woollen ground, using brightly coloured crewel wools.

57 (below). Bedspread: Westover-Berkeley. North America,
c. 1740
Richmond, Va. : Valentine Museum

The Westover-Berkeley coverlet is a supreme example of
appliqué work. It was made by the ladies of two families, the
Byrds and the Harrisons, who lived on the adjoining
plantations of Westover and Berkeley in Virginia. It has a
beautiful and elaborate design based on squares and triangles,
using pieces cut from chintz supplemented with embroidery.
It is the extreme delicacy and fineness of the motifs, and the
neatness and skill with which the intricate shapes have been
applied, which compel admiration. The baskets are made
from ribbon attached with buttonhole stitch.

58 (right) Candlewick spread. U.S.A., *c.* 1810
Philadelphia: Museum of Art (Titus C. Geesey collection)

In this bedspread, candlewick cotton has been used to
embroider the design in two sizes of French knots. Designs
for this type of work have to be clear and simple, and this
one with its baskets and vases of meandering flowers and its
border of swags is appropriate and charming. In plates 69 and
70 other swags, worked at about the same time, may be
compared; but embroidery for French palaces is a far cry
from work for a typical American home.

59 (below): Long pillow bere. England, late sixteenth century
London: Victoria and Albert Museum

This cover is one of a set of four and is among the most
perfect pieces of Elizabethan embroidery that remain. It has
all the hallmarks of its period: the curling stems enclosing
flowers and fruit; a preoccupation with gardening and the old
and new plants available; a dislike of empty spaces in the
design,-and a marvellous sense of the right stitch and colour
for the subject. Bright silks and metal threads are used on a
ground of white linen and the stitches have been chosen to
emphasize the character of each flower: chain, square double
chain, stem, plaited braid, and buttonhole, with the addition
of some fillings.

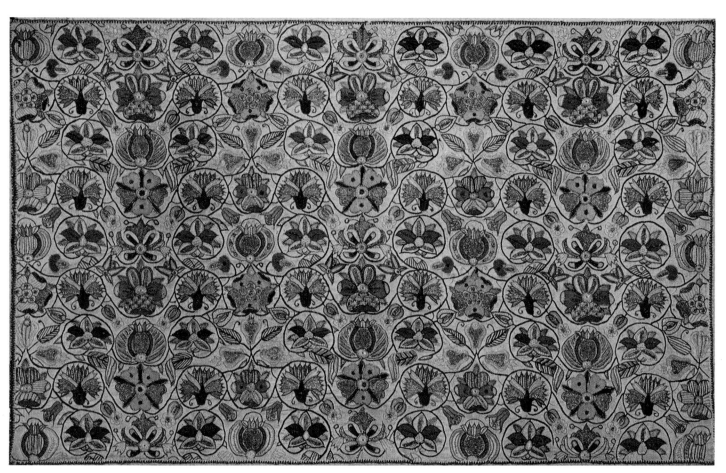

60: Coat. India, first half of the seventeenth century
London: Victoria and Albert Museum

This splendid coat is worked in chain stitch on satin rather
than the more usual cotton, in a design incorporating
hillocks, flowering trees, animals, plants, birds, butterflies,
and other insects. It is dated between 1628 and 1658, that is
from the time of the Mogul emperor Shah Jehan. The
Moguls, especially the Shah's father Akbar the Great, were
very interested in all the arts and brought craftsmen from
Persia to work alongside the Indians in workshops or
khirkanas. The result, especially in work from northern
India, is a blend of the two cultures which is particularly
evident in this coat.

61 (right): Pair of gloves. Netherlands, *c.* 1630
Munich: Bayerisches Museum

This pair of gloves belonged to Elizabeth Stuart, daughter of
James I of England, who married the Elector Frederick V of
the Palatine in 1613. The gauntlets are beautifully and
professionally embroidered using coloured silks with pearls,
the design showing that mixture of naturalism and formalism
so typical of the period.

   It is considered that these gloves were made in the
Netherlands about 1630 and were probably a present to
Elizabeth. Gloves were frequently given as New Year presents
which explains why so many have been preserved, apparently
unworn, and this pair probably comes into that category.

62 (right): Christening gown. North
Germany, *c.* 1700
Hamburg: Museum fur Kunst und Gewerbe

The technique of whitework has always been a
speciality of central European countries,
mainly north and south Germany, Austria
and Switzerland. They were, or were near,
flax growing areas and so could obtain
supplies of linen and threads; and being
Protestant countries they were not so much
engaged in the making of rich ecclesiastical
vestments. The whitework of this christening
gown is a splendid mixture of surface
stitchery, pulled fabric stitches and quilting —
a mixture which might have become fussy if it
were not restrained by the discipline of the
monochrome colouring.

63 (above): Woman's hood. English, late sixteenth century
London: Victoria and Albert Museum

Blackwork was one of the outstanding techniques of the
sixteenth century in England. Like so many other forms of
embroidery it originated in the East, and was then brought to
Spain by the Arabs after which it made its way to England,
probably in the fourteenth century.

Black silk with, occasionally, a metal passing thread, was
used on white linen, with a number of different flat stitches
and filling patterns. The hood illustrated, dating from the late
sixteenth century, has a design of flowers within coiling stems
which may be compared with that of the woman's jacket
(plate 66) and the pillow bere (plate 59).

65 (right): Lady's dress (detail). China, c. 1720
Stockholm: Nordiska Museum

To the European there have always been three facets of
Chinese ambroidery: firstly, the superb pieces worked by the
Chinese for their own use; secondly, the embroideries worked
by the Chinese to the European taste and according to
European designs; and lastly, chinoiserie — which is not
Chinese at all, but the European idea of Chinese work.

The gown of which the lower part of the skirt is illustrated
belongs to the second category. It was worked about 1720 in
China to a design then popular in England, which was sent
out to China to be copied.

To our eyes the gold embroidery worked over parchment
might perhaps have been done in Europe, but the flowers
with their rows of satin stitch becoming darker towards the
centre, and the delightfully clear gap between each row, could
not possibly be other than Chinese.

64 (above): Mocassin. Huron Indian tribe, c. 1830
Oxford: Pitt Rivers Museum

In 1639 five Ursuline nuns were sent from France to found a
convent in Quebec. At first they taught embroidery to Indian
and French-Canadian pupils using the conventional silk and
metal threads, but because of the difficulty of obtaining
supplies they eventually turned to moosehair, which had been
used by the Indians as thread for many years.

In the mocassin illustrated small bundles of moosehair
were laid on to the line to be worked and were couched down
with a thread which was pulled very tight, almost giving the
effect of small beads.

66: Lady's jacket. England, late sixteenth century
London: Victoria and Albert Museum

The type of garment illustrated was worn throughout the late sixteenth and early seventeenth centuries, and was sometimes decorated with blackwork but more often, as in this superb specimen, worked in bright silks with silver and gilt threads on linen. The design is that favourite of the sixteenth century, the coiling stem with flowers, fruit and leaves, symmetrically but informally embroidered all over the garment. Each coil is of one plant only, with each flower in a different stage of development. The pea, for example, has the pods open and closed, and the flower of the pea at the end of the coil. The jacket is simply worked in chain and buttonhole stitches.

67 (below): Hanging. U.S.S.R., Nineteenth century
Paris: Musée de l'Homme

The cotton hanging illustrated comes from Bokhara in
Uzbekistan and there are resemblances to Persian and Indian
embroideries in the strength of the circular flowers contrasted
with the more formal leaves. The design is divided up in a
way very reminiscent of a tiled floor.
   The hanging is worked in Bokhara couching, a stitch that
uses the tying down thread irregularly. This gives the work a
solid appearance, as there is no play of light and shade.

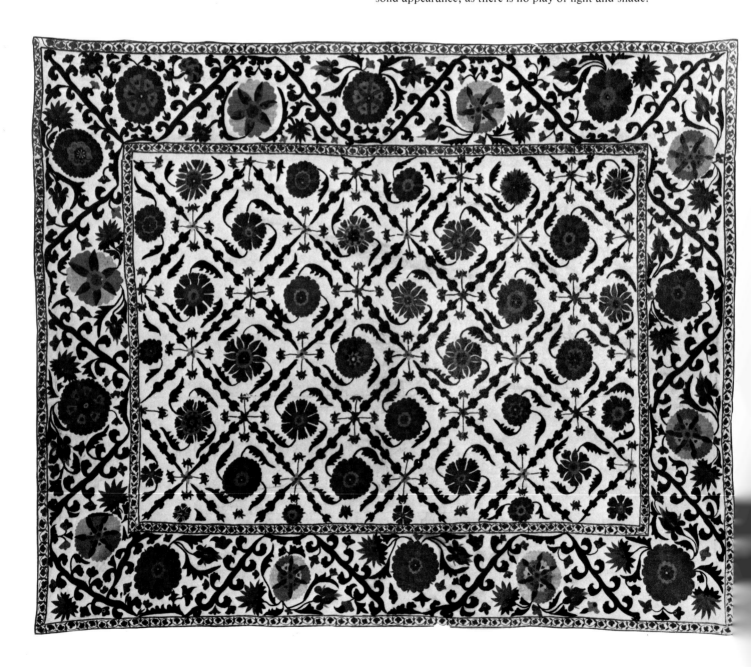

68 (right): *Hatton Garden hanging*. England, second half of the seventeenth century
London: Victoria and Albert Museum

The second half of the seventeenth century was notable for crewel work curtains worked mainly in stem and chain stitches with a variety of filling stitches; but these hangings (found in a house in Hatton Garden, London, in the 1890s) while using the crewel wools which must have been obtainable in abundance, are worked in a wide variety of canvas stitches — tent, brick, cross, crosslet and rococo. It is seldom that such an informal design is worked in stitches which are so formal. The prancing horse at the foot of the design may be compared with the prancing horse in the other, very different, English crewel work hanging illustrated in plate 32.

69 and 70: Wall hanging (whole and detail). France, 1804-15
Paris: Musée National de la Maison

The Musée National de la Maison holds lengths of fabrics
which have been used to decorate the French royal palaces:
this is one of them, a wall covering in pristine condition
worked in coloured silks and gold threads by the firm of
Biscardon, Bony et Cie about 1810. From the time of Louis
XIV onwards, whenever there were new wall or seat coverings
ordered for a royal residence, extra fabrics were woven or
embroidered to be used when necessary as replacements. A
piece on this scale makes one wonder how many embroiderers
would have had to work for how long to create enough
hangings for one large salon.

71 (above): Wall hanging. England, *c.* 1720
National Trust: Montacute House

To the social historian two hangings from Stoke
Edith in Herefordshire are of great interest as they
show the formal gardens of the time, and also the
way these gardens were used and enjoyed by the
owners of the house. Plants and fountains, orange
trees on the balustrade, dogs, children, a monkey
picking a flower, a footman tripping and falling
down the steps, a family having tea round a tripod
table — all are faithfully represented in tent stitch.
These panels are representative of the many which
were worked by the ladies of the house, with their
relations, attendant gentlewomen, and hired
helpers, to decorate and enhance their homes.

72 (right): The Magic Garden. England, 1937
London: Victoria and Albert Museum

At the start of the twentieth century the idea that a
design should be illustrated and enhanced by
appropriate, rather than conventional, stitches
came into being; and after the First World War,
and especially by the 1930s, economy of both time
and materials became necessary.
    This panel of 1937 worked by Rebecca
Crompton epitomizes contemporary thinking. The
techniques are simple and quick — applique with
surface stitches freely worked — and the materials
are few and cheap. The design and stitches
complement each other so exactly that it is
impossible to visualize one without the other.

73 (left): Pincushion. England, early seventeenth century
London: Victoria and Albert Museum

In the Middle Ages pins were widely used for fastening clothes; they were scarce and expensive, so it became important to have large cushions in which they could be stuck for safe keeping. This example from the early seventeenth century uses tent and gobelin stitches with some French knots. The work is done on an extremely fine linen canvas using a silk thread.

74 (below): Sofa upholstery. England, 1743-48
Port Sunlight: Lady Lever Art Gallery

By the eighteenth century comfort in all types of seating was acceptable, normal, and even insisted upon. Wing chairs, padded window seats, upholstered sofas, and many cushions, were to be seen in all houses with any pretensions to gentility. Various techniques were used, but most covers were embroidered with wool on canvas using tent or cross stitch. In the eighteenth century embroidered furniture would be protected by loose covers unless company was expected, and this has helped to prolong the life of the work.

The three-seat sofa illustrated evidently took more than five years to work, as the seat is dated Sept 27th 1743, and the back Dec 17th 1748. The cover is worked in cross stitch in crewel wool with a design of large, rampant flowers and foliage.

75 (right): Vase of Flowers. Holland, 1650
Amsterdam: Rijksmuseum

This picture, embroidered in *or nué* by Wynent Haelwech in 1650, is exactly like a Dutch flower painting of the same date. All the ingredients are there: the glass vase crammed with spring flowers, the loose petals on the table, and the delicate colouring.

76: Prayer carpet. Persia, nineteenth century
London: Victoria and Albert Museum

This type of applied work evolved at the small town of Resht
on the Caspian Sea and is not quite like any other kind of
applique. The designs are cut out of coloured cloth and applied
to a cloth ground, after which each piece is outlined with cord
or chain stitch, with added stitchery where necessary.

77: Military tent (detail). Poland, eighteenth century
Cracow: Wawel Castle, State art Collection

From the middle of the sixteenth to the end of the seventeenth
centuries the Turks overran a considerable part of south-east
Europe, and were constantly fighting with the Poles. From
time to time the Poles captured richly embroidered horse
trappings and military tents from the Turks, and acquired a
taste for such things. They imported tents from Persia and
Turkey, and also made them in Poland, using Armenian and
Jewish embroideries. This explains why the design of this tent
is based on Turkish shapes but is not entirely Persian, Turkish,
nor Polish. The technique used is cotton appliqué on linen.

78: Rug. England, 1743
New York: Metropolitan Museum of Art (gift of Irwin
Untermyer)

This rug is worked in coloured wools on canvas in cross stitch
and the shape of the very florid design is basically Oriental in
conception, though there is no hint of chinoiserie. The
scalloped diamond in the centre with the four corner shapes is
a form seen in many Persian càrpets and in prayer rugs. The
riot of flowers and foliage, however, is anything but Oriental;
while the soft pinks, reds, blues and golds are the epitome of
an English garden.

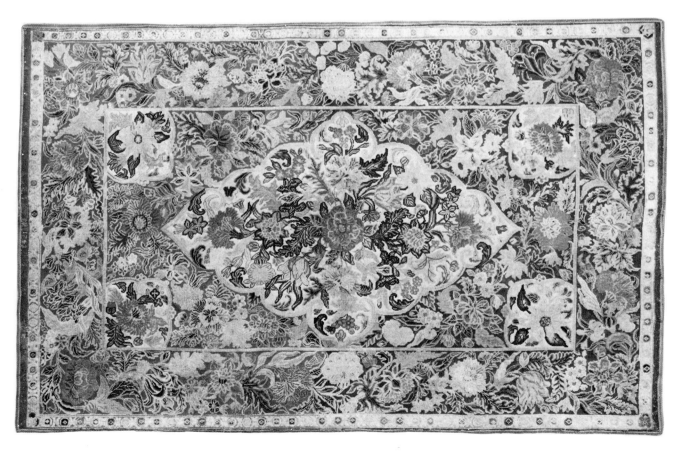

79: Rug. England, *c*. 1750
New York: Brooklyn Museum

This is worked in cross stitch in rich colours and
although it has been dated to about 1750 the
elements of the design, especially the border, appear
rather earlier. The large flowers — though arranged
more formally — are the flowers seen in the
seventeenth century, and the whole design speaks of
the talented amateur rather than the professional.